ZiGGY'S Friends for Life

by Tom Wilson

A 30th ANNIVERSARY TRIBUTE TO ZIG FROM ALL OF HIS FRIENDS.

**Andrews McMeel
Publishing**

Kansas City

www.uexpress.com and www.andrewsmcmeel.com

01 02 03 04 05 BAH 10 9 8 7 6 5 4 3 2 1

ISBN: 0-7407-1605-0

Library of Congress Catalog Card Number: 00-108967

— **ATTENTION: SCHOOLS AND BUSINESSES** —

Andrews McMeel books are available at quantity discounts with bulk purchase for educational, business, or sales promotional use. For information, please write to: Special Sales Department, Andrews McMeel Publishing, 4520 Main Street, Kansas City, Missouri 64111.

This book is dedicated to the loving memory of Susan Wilson.

1971–1980

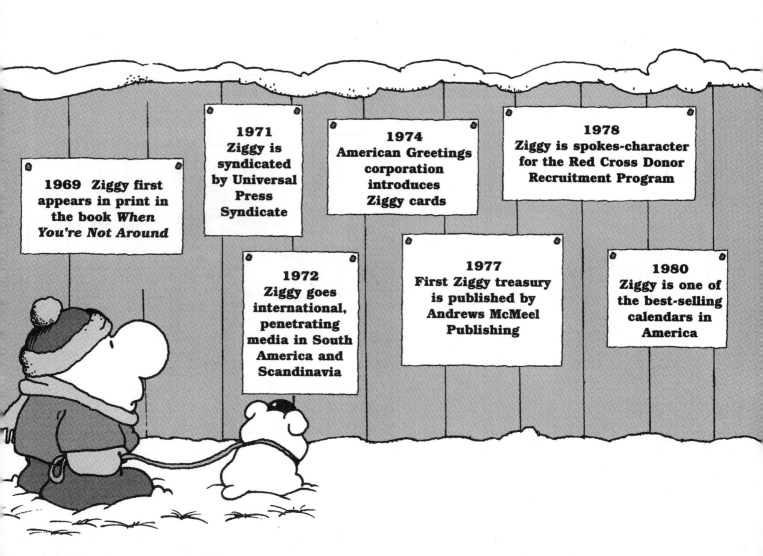

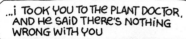

1981–1990

1981
Ziggy and Tom Wilson are interviewed by Gene Shalit on the *Today* show

1982
Ziggy appears in the animated Christmas special, *Ziggy's Gift* and wins the Emmy for Outstanding Animation

1983
Ziggy first appears on leukemia coinboard

1984
Ziggy is awarded the World Hunger Media Award for support of World Food Day

1985
Tom Wilson establishes his own licensing company, Ziggy and Friends, Inc.

1985
Tom Wilson's son, Tom II, begins drawing Ziggy and joins Ziggy and Friends as Vice President

1987
Ziggy sells 50 million greeting cards annually

...WHEW! JOSH'S CAGE WAS A MESS TODAY!

...IT TOOK ME OVER A HALF HOUR TO CLEAN IT!!

...THERE WERE SEEDS, HULLS EVERY-WHERE! SPILLED WATER, FEATHERS ALL OVER THE FLOOR OF THE CAGE!

...NOT EVEN TO MENTION THE UNMENTIONABLE STUFF! HOO BOY!!

ANYWAY... I DON'T KNOW HOW ONE BIRD CAN MAKE SUCH A MESS! G'NIGHT, FUZZ!

click

GIMME TWO, FREDDIE. HEY, THERE'S PLENTY OF EATS, GUYS!

NICE PLACE, JOSH

I'M IN!

73

1995
Ziggy cards introduced by Hallmark

1996
The animated Christmas special *Ziggy's Gift* debuts in Japan

1997
Ziggy's appointed spokes-character for the "Woman's Life" section of *Woman's World* magazine.

1998
Ziggy's chosen as spokes-character by the New York City Department of Transportation for Bicycle Month

1995
Ziggy appears in ads for the hair product Rogaine

1998
Ziggy is spokes-character for the California Secretary of State's Voter Outreach Program

1998
Ziggy appears as a parade balloon in Philadelphia's Thanksgiving Day Parade

1998
Ziggy mentioned in episodes of *Seinfeld*, *Caroline in the City*, and *The Tonight Show*

1991–2000

1999
Ziggy debuts in Toon Lagoon, one of five "Islands of Adventure" in Universal Studios theme park in Orlando, Florida

1999
Ziggy featured in special Dodge Motor Company campaign at 140 locations in the World Trade Center, New York City

2000
Ziggy debuts in his very own Web site, www.ziggyzone.com

1999
Ziggy makes cartoon history with the Great Aspirations arctic expedition as the first cartoon character to reach the North Pole

1999
First cover book on Ziggy memorabilia is published—*The Unauthorized Guide to Ziggy Collectibles* by Andrea Campbell

2000
Ziggy cards introduced by Recycled Paper Greetings, Inc.

... ZIG, DID YOU KNOW YOUR LIPS MOVE WHEN YOU READ?

SO WHAT.... EVEN EDGAR BERGEN'S LIPS MOVED WHEN HE DID CHARLIE McCARTHY! ...BESIDES, LOTS OF FOLK'S LIPS MOVE WHEN THEY READ!!

...YEH, BUT, GUESS WHAT, ZIG...

...YOUR LIPS EVEN MOVE WHEN YOU **THINK!**

BOY... TOMORROW IS VALENTINE'S DAY, ... A DAY TO REMEMBER SOMEONE YOU LOVE!

AND HERE I AM WITH NOBODY TO BUY A CARD AND CANDY FOR.

SIGH

THANK GOODNESS I PICKED UP DOG YUMMIE, CATNIP, SUNFLOWER SEEDS, GOLDFISH FOOD AND JIFFY POP ON THE WAY HOME...

I'm such a close pal of Ziggy's that I'm one of his few friends allowed to call him Zyzzyva. Mostly, because I'm one of his few friends who can pronounce it.

(We have a private joke: "See no weevil, hear no weevil, speak no weevil," because Ziggy knows what Zyzzyva means.)

For some 30 years Ziggy has delighted the world. Ziggy is invariably witty, clever, amusing, philosophical, wise, hilarious—an all-around pleasure.

Namely, he's a wonderful pleasure to be around.

Cheers to Tom Wilson and Tom Too.

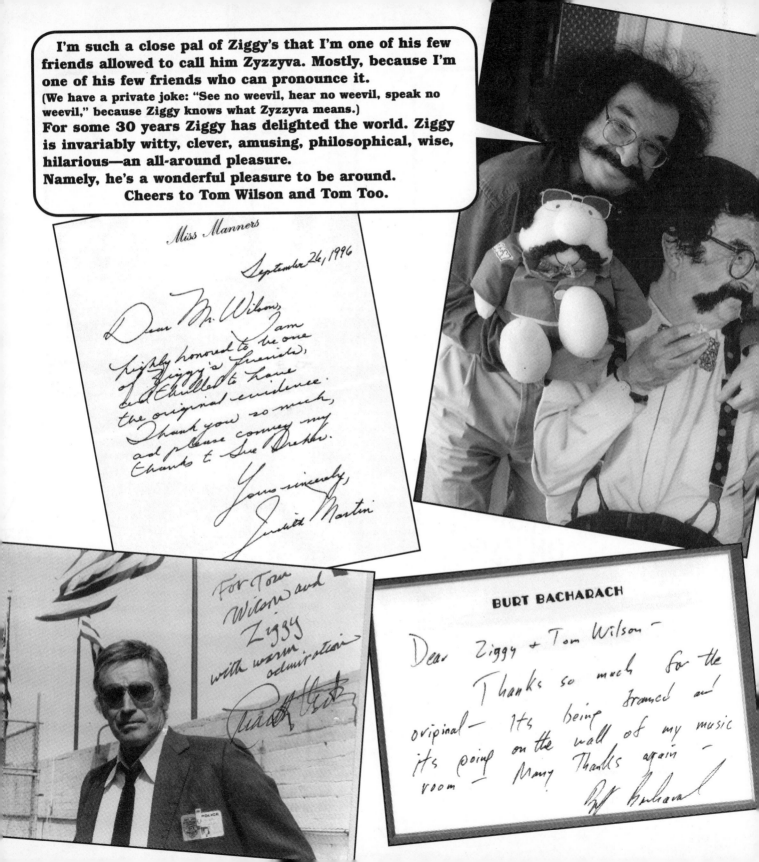

Miss Manners

September 26, 1996

Dear Mr. Wilson, I am highly honored to be one of Ziggy's friends, and thrilled to have the original evidence. Thank you so much, and please convey my thanks to Sue Dreher.

Yours sincerely,

Judith Martin

For Tom Wilson and Ziggy with warm admiration

BURT BACHARACH

Dear Ziggy & Tom Wilson—
Thanks so much for the original— It's being framed and it's going on the wall of my music room— Many Thanks again—

Bf Bacharach